Do You Take God? *Workbook*

Eric L. Owens

Printed in the United States of America

10 9 8 7 6 5 4 3 2 1

Contents

From The Author

Thank you,

For your marriage and your commitment to God. It was not good that the man was alone, so God made a woman; in marriage you should never again be alone. But, the blessings of marriage are hard to appreciate when viewed through the lens of challenge and crisis.

As we learned in "Do you take God" issues are made worse if we have an improper view of marriage. The picture we are painted of marriage as children is so terribly untrue. Our expectations of each other based on a misrepresentation often create challenges that are exceedingly difficult to overcome.

This workbook is designed to help put into practice the things we learned in the book. Each chapter has a series of questions. These questions are asked to further thought and discussion about the content in the chapter. Reference to the book is necessary to answer the questions. This will also serve as a reminder of the things learned.

The questions are not intended to be used as weapons against each other. Rather, they are intended to promote open and honest discussion. By creating dialogue about our concerns we can more clearly hear and see each other's point of view. Such an experience will also help us effectively develop a plan of action to resolve our challenges.

Following the questsions there is an exercise that you can do. Learning is important but learning is only useful if we practice what we've learned. Jesus told the apostles that they needed to know the things he taught them. But he added, "happy are you if you do them" (John 13:17). Some exercises are for husbands and others are for wives and some are for both.

The key is doing. Following the example of Jesus, humility, forgiveness and service are essential for Christians. Let this mind be in you which was also in Christ Jesus (Philippians 2:5-7). No greater life can be lived than to follow the example of Jesus. And no greater marriage will ever be enjoyed, than two people learning of God, living like Christ and loving each other.

May God bless your marriage and may your marriage be a blessing to you and to others.

In Christian love,

Eric

Chapter One

We Can't Actually Redefine Marriage

DISCUSSION QUESTIONS:

1. Give a definition of marriage as you understand it. Is your definition the same as God's?

2. Does objective truth exist or is everything subjective, explain and give examples of both?

3. Is defining marriage like choosing burger chains, can you have it your way?

4. What are some implications of us seeking to redefine marriage?

5. If there is no objective standard or definition for marriage how else can it be redefined?

6. Is homosexuality like being black? If it is what else could one say is like being black that is also referred to as a sin in scripture?

7. If marriage is "redefined" one way, what are some other ways it can be "redefined?"

8. Explain Acts 5:29 in light of the Supreme Court's decision on marriage.

9. What are some implications for marriage if we do away with gender distinctions?

10. Discuss some ways marriage will be affected in the future because of this "redefinition."

Exercise

As a family, do an exercise where you identify things and define them. Does your family use identity as an important feature of life? Does your family rely on the certainty of definitions everyday? If you have children teach them how important this part of life is (Deuteronomy 6:4-13). Ask each member to describe marriage and how it works.

NOTES

NOTES

Chapter Two

What Is Marriage - Can You Describe It?

DISCUSSION QUESTIONS:

1. Where did you get the ideas you have about marriage?

2. What do you believe is the most disappointing thing about marriage?

3. What do you believe is the best part of marriage?

4. What can you do to bring your expectations in line with God's intentions?

5. Did anyone adequately prepare you for marriage, can they?

6. How was marriage modeled before you and how does that affect you?

7. Did your expectations meet what God intended?

8. What is your definition of marriage?

9. How much of your energy was spent on what you were getting into when you got married versus what God intended when he gave us marriage?

10. If a young person asked you about marriage, what would you tell them?

Exercise:

Write down what you thought you were getting into when you got married. Then swap papers and discuss. Use this as an opportunity to share your rearing, experiences and thoughts about marriage. Unmet expectations are a major disappointment and difficulty in marriage. Use what you learn to be more merciful and understanding with each other.

NOTES

NOTES

Chapter Three

God's Design For Marriage - Design Determines Function.

DISCUSSION QUESTIONS:

1. How would you explain God's design for marriage as portrayed in the garden?

2. Do you agree or disagree with God's design of male leadership? Explain.

3. If not male leadership, what is the design of marriage?

4. Practically, what does a leaderless marriage look like?

5. Are role distinctions the beginning of the problems in marriage?

6. Discuss your understanding of the phrase, "Wives submit to your husbands."

7. Why isn't the language of submission ever reversed?

8. What did God mean to Eve when he said, "He will rule over you?"

9. Does a woman need to understand submission before she gets married?

10. Who designed the roles? Who is she submitting to and who calls her to submit?

Exercise:

Each person choose an organization. It can be a business, charity, government, sports organization or anything. Review and discuss its organizational structure. How can any organization function without a leader? Discuss those leaders and then God's organization of the home.

NOTES

NOTES

Chapter Four

Applying God's Design Beyond Marriage

DISCUSSION QUESTIONS:

1. Share your thoughts about the design of leadership in other areas of life: government to citizens, elders to members, parents to children or bosses to employees.

2. Do you agree that those under the leadership of others should submit?

3. Does the design of male leadership apply in a marriage? If so- why? If not, why not?

4. If it's not the design of male leadership in marriage, what design for marriage should we follow?

5. How can we explain leadership when we are in charge in other areas of life and dismiss it in marriage?

6. If it can work in other areas without being abused, why can't it work in marriage without abuse?

7. Explain what you believe God intended with the words he chose and examples he gave in the Bible, rule over, submit to and others.

8. How successful will we be in marriage if we go against God's design?

9. Do you think God made us unique and different to fulfill the roles he gave us? Explain.

10. Are you and your spouse in the roles God designed for you?

Exercise:

Pray together for a week asking God to help each of you fulfill your role to him and for him, according to his design. Our marriages are as much about us and God as they are about us.

NOTES

NOTES

Chapter Five

Flag On The Play - You've Gone Too Far

DISCUSSION QUESTIONS:

1. Has male leadership become a myth?
2. Explain our change from "he shall rule over you" to "happy wife happy life."
3. What effects have our changes had on our marriages?
4. Are women leading the home or are men?
5. Has he become a help meet for her?
6. What are our children learning from our marriages?
7. Are husbands silent supporters or spiritual leaders?
8. Can we understand male leadership like the other areas of leadership?
9. How would you want someone to respond to you if you were the manager, parent, etc?
10. Discuss the phrases, "she has her say" "the husband is the head, the wife is the neck" "if mama's not happy, no one is happy."

Exercise:

Research society's view of the male in the home. Consider television shows, movies and other media forms. Has society convinced us that women are smarter, more capable leaders and that men are just big dumb boys? How has this impacted our marriages and view of male leadership?

NOTES

NOTES

Chapter Six

No One Has The Right To Sin Against God

DISCUSSION QUESTIONS:

1. Should we acknowledge our own sin against God before we address sins against us?
2. Describe how awful your sin is to God.
3. Are you willing to accept the sentence due for sin from God or do you want forgiveness?
4. How does God forgiving us impact us forgiving others?
5. What is God's position toward us if we refuse to forgive those who've sinned against us?
6. Are you willing to emulate God's actions toward you when others sin against you?
7. Discuss the three fold view of Isaiah 6:1-5, upward, inward and outward?
8. Should someone sinning against us be greater than our sinning against God?
9. Do you keep a record of sins against you, while wanting complete forgiveness when you sin?
10. Are your present actions toward your spouse sinful actions toward God?

Exercise:

Study the word sin, look at examples and study how God acted toward those who sinned against him. Consider the ultimate sacrifice of Christ on the cross and God's willingness to forgive those who murdered his son. Recommit to your relationship with God, reconnect with each other, pray with each other and for each other.

NOTES

NOTES

Chapter Seven

Heaven Presents - Woman

DISCUSSION QUESTIONS:

1. What did God see in the garden with Adam?
2. What did God say about Adam being alone?
3. Who solved Adam's issue and what does Luke 3:38 have to do with it?
4. According to Genesis 2, how should husbands think of their wives?
5. What comes along with headship?
6. What three things are involved in receiving a gift? Apply that to your wife.
7. What is the basis of a woman's worth?
8. What did Eve have to do to earn her place?
9. What three connections did Eve have to Adam?
10. Why should husbands, in particular, read Genesis 2 with fresh eyes?

Exercise:

Research the same media outlets and see how women are portrayed. How has the exploitation of women affected men's thoughts and behavior toward women? Men for twenty-one days verbally affirm your wife. Don't just tell her she is, share with her why you think she is wonderful. According to the chapter, she is Heaven's gift. Examine your heart and pray to God that you treat her the way God intends. Are the women in your life treated like a gift from God?

NOTES

NOTES

Chapter Eight

Christ: The Second Adam

DISCUSSION QUESTIONS:

1. Adam and Eve are represented by who in the New Testament?
2. Discuss the meaning and significance of Christ as the second Adam?
3. Who is the standard and example for every husband's behavior toward his wife?
4. A husband's behavior toward his wife is not based on her actions; explain?
5. What things did Paul say Christ was to the church?
6. What does that mean about husbands and wives?
7. What one word would you use to describe how Christ treated the church?
8. Christ died for his bride how should this impact husbands?
9. Can a husband please God if he does not love his wife like Christ loved the church?
10. Explain a husband's faithfulness to his wife, how does that relate to Christ?

Exercise:

After the twenty-one days of affirmation, for the next twenty-one days do something to help your wife. Her load is often heavy, she juggles many things. Do something to lighten her load and make it easier on her. Have fun, rub her feet, help clean the house, take the children out, give her a massage, be creative.

NOTES

NOTES

Chapter Nine

God's Word To Those Who Lead

DISCUSSION QUESTIONS:

1. What two things are involved in leadership?
2. What does God's conversation with Adam teach us?
3. Give specifics of God's expectations of leaders.
4. What kind of husbands does God expect?
5. Who is responsible for being a good husband? Explain.
6. My failure to be what God wants will have what effect on my marriage?
7. How will blaming my spouse explain, affect or improve my marriage?
8. Are God's expectations of leaders too great?
9. Are husband's souls at stake based on their behavior as husbands?
10. How can a husband get help if he has not led as God expects?

Exercise:

Search the Bible for good leaders, then find five traits or qualities that made them successful. Discuss and see which ones can be implemented in your marriage. Pray for the success of the leader in your home.

NOTES

NOTES

Chapter Ten

My Wife Won't Reverence Me - What Can I Do?

DISCUSSION QUESTIONS:

1. Explain your position on reverence, what does it mean to you?
2. Are there acceptable reasons from God why a wife doesn't have to reverence her husband?
3. If there are acceptable reasons what are they?
4. If a wife doesn't reverence her husband, how should she treat him?
5. If God holds us to the vows we made, how does that impact reverence?
6. Instead of quitting, what should a husband who is not reverenced do?
7. Are our actions justified by our spouse's actions? If not, what should a husband do?
8. How can one's relationship with God help him if he feels he is being done wrong?
9. Discuss your thoughts on liking your spouse and loving them?
10. How long do you want to carry around the pain, hurt and anger from the past? Be specific.

Exercise:

Sit and write down how you have treated your wife. Be specific about how you have spoken to her, what you said as well as tone. List any projects that she has requested to be done that remain undone. Note how you have helped around the house and with the children. This should encompass a significant enough time to show a pattern of behavior. Now if what you wrote was not how God would have you lead and act toward her, commit the next 60 days to changing it.

NOTES

NOTES

Chapter Eleven

What She Means When She Says "You Don't Love Me."

DISCUSSION QUESTIONS:

1. Explain Malachi 1:6-8. How does this relate to a husband loving his wife?
2. Is saying 'I love you' the same as loving your wife?
3. Explain your view of whether or not a husband must earn his wife's respect?
4. What does "husband love your wife" look like in practice to you?
5. If a wife has to earn love or can stop being loved, how does that apply to reverence?
6. Do you love your wife?
7. Should every wife have what Eve and the church had with Adam and Christ?
8. How can a wife be assured she is preeminent in her husband's life?
9. Discuss the meaning and implications of the word "regard" for one's wife.
10. Explain your story, is it being written together; are you one with your wife or are you two?

Exercise:

Sit and write down how you have treated your husband. Be specific about how you have listened to him. Consider how you've talked to him, what you said as well as tone. List any decisions he has made with which you disagreed or didn't follow. Note your attitude toward sex, his arrival at home or general approach to him. This should encompass a significant enough time to show a pattern of behavior. Now if what you wrote was not how God would have you follow and act toward him, commit the next 60 days to changing it.

NOTES

NOTES

Chapter Twelve

God Cares For Women

DISCUSSION QUESTIONS:

1. What things did God do that demonstrate his care for women?
2. What was God's intention from the beginning for marriage?
3. Why should we keep ourselves until marriage?
4. How did Christ elevate women?
5. God did not prevent men from sinning but he often regulated their action. How did he do that in Israel concerning marriage?
6. How does God tell a man to treat his wife?
7. Does being the head of a woman demand abuse of a woman?
8. Is the problem God's design or man's disobedience in following God's design?
9. If we change God's plan, how will that demonstrate his care for women?
10. Discuss the importance of caring for yourself in the pursuit of a spouse.

Exercise:

Site specific instances in history where we did not follow God's design. Discuss how this could affect a woman's view of male leadership. Discuss solutions to the problem without changing God's design. Are women treated with honor and respect in your home, church or community?

NOTES

NOTES

Chapter Thirteen

Why God Gave Leadership

DISCUSSION QUESTIONS:

1. How does a better understanding of leadership help the one who leads?
2. How does a better understanding of leadership help those who are led?
3. Explain God's use of leadership knowing abuse could happen.
4. How does God's call of Moses to lead Israel help husbands lead their wives?
5. How should a wife feel about being led by her husband? How do you?
6. Who is a wife's greatest ally in the role she is in and why?
7. What are leaders to provide for those they lead?
8. Discuss your thoughts of leadership. How do they compare with God's?
9. Discuss the idea that the one looking most intently at the leader's work is God.
10. Should a husband seek to solve his wife's problems? Why or why not?

Exercise:

Have a Bible study and pray nightly with your family. Read through the Bible and find faithful leaders. Look at their strengths and weakness. Involve your children and teach that everyone is a leader in some way: husbands and wives, mothers and children and older siblings to younger siblings. Focus on God as being the leader of us all (1 Corinthians 11:3; Ephesians 5:23-25; Ephesians 6:1-4).

NOTES

NOTES

Chapter Fourteen

God's Word To Those Who Follow

DISCUSSION QUESTIONS:

1. Who established the roles?
2. Explain why a wife's actions toward her husband are not about her husband.
3. Give specifics about what God says to followers.
4. What can be learned from the other spheres of followers?
5. What is the wife's example and who is she to emulate?
6. If a wife is not behaving as she should what can she do to get help?
7. What excuses can be made for our individual actions in marriage?
8. Can a wife's soul be in jeopardy because of her actions in her marriage?
9. What does Israel's interaction with Moses teach wives today?
10. Are God's expectations of wives too great?

Exercise:

Find examples in the Bible of great followers. Write down five traits or characteristics that made them successful. How can you emulate them and put them into practice in your home? Pray for the success of those who follow in your home.

NOTES

NOTES

Chapter Fifteen

My Husband Won't Lead Me What Can I Do?

DISCUSSION QUESTIONS:

1. Discuss your prayer life. How can it be strengthened? What do you believe prayer can do?
2. If a wife's husband won't lead, what would be the most damaging thing she could do?
3. Discuss your Bible study, meditation and time of reflection with God's word.
4. Does God guide all areas of your life? Seriously consider your whole life's walk with God.
5. Does anyone intend to love, honor and cherish if we experience the worst in our marriage?
6. How can self examinations help husbands and wives (2 Corinthians 13:5)?
7. How can comparing ourselves to Jesus and not each other help us (1 Peter 2:21-25)?
8. What does it mean to have the mind of Christ for husbands and wives (Philippians 2:1-7)?
9. Discuss hope, what is it, what does it mean, how does it apply to your life?
10. Discuss how the actions of your spouse affects your actions.

Exercise:

Hold hands every day. Look each other in the eye and talk every day. Write a note to your wife expressing your love to her everyday. Express your love and commitment to each other. Do this for twenty-one days.

NOTES

NOTES

Chapter Sixteen

What He Means When He Says - You Don't Respect Me

DISCUSSION QUESTIONS:

1. Explain your understanding of respect in our culture.

2. Explain your understanding of reverence in Scripture.

3. How does "earning respect" affect reverencing your husband?

4. Discuss David's actions toward Saul, what does that tell us about reverence?

5. Discuss the difference between a husband coming home a generation ago and today.

6. Explain Malachi 1:6-8, how does this relate to husbands and wives?

7. Is saying what one does not do to her husband the same as reverence?

8. Explain your view of whether or not a husband must earn his wife's respect.

9. What does reverence look like in practice to you?

10. If a husband has to earn reverence does a wife have to earn love? Explain Ephesians 5:33.

Exercise:

First, she needs to read Colossians 3:12-18 and 1 Peter 3:1-6. A wife needs to focus on her relationship with Christ and God and not her husband. Live with your husband as if he were Christ. How would you treat him, talk to him, approach him and show your love and respect to him?

NOTES

NOTES

Chapter Seventeen

What Is Love?

DISCUSSION QUESTIONS:

1. Is it fair to say we love, love?
2. Discuss the two views of love, and the merits of each.
3. How does the world's view of love differ from the definitions?
4. What would you say to a young person who says, "I've fallen in love"?
5. Do you love your spouse?
6. Discuss each phrase of 1 Corinthians 13:1-8.
7. According to 1 Corinthians 13, Love is greater than what things?
8. What can we learn from God about love?
9. Discuss this thought: Every other problem in marriage is ultimately a love problem.
10. How can love end if love never ceases?

Exercise:

Love affirms. Affirm your love for your spouse everyday. Love serves. Do a kind deed for your spouse beyond what you normally do. Take the time and think about something they would enjoy or appreciate. Love considers. Ask your spouse about their feelings and what you can do to help. Think, speak and act love toward and for your spouse everyday for the rest of your life.

NOTES

NOTES

Chapter Eighteen

Learning To Forgive Like God

DISCUSSION QUESTIONS:

1. Write out a Bible definition of forgiveness.
2. List some things about how God forgives.
3. What is essential for forgiveness to occur (Luke 17:3)?
4. Define and explain repentance.
5. Discuss the difference between repentance and forgiveness, which part belongs to you?
6. In your estimation, what is the goal of forgiveness?
7. Why does the Scripture emphasize forgiving quickly? Discuss Ephesians 4:26-27.
8. How does reading and understanding Matthew 6:14-15 make you feel?
9. This chapter wasn't about repentance it was about forgiveness, what does that mean?
10. Discuss your sin against God and the outcome of Matthew 18:21-35.

Exercise:

Have a forgiveness and release ceremony. Take the pain you have been carrying with you and write it down. You can burn it, throw it away or do any symbolic gesture you see fit. But you must release it and free yourself from it. You have carried it too long, it has cost you too much pain and ruined too many days. God has forgiven you so he is never bound by your wrong. Read Psalm 103 and practice it in your life. Pray to God and, once and for all, feel the burden lifted.

NOTES

NOTES

Chapter Nineteen

Ten Tips For Husbands And Wives

DISCUSSION QUESTIONS:

1. Which tip did you not know your spouse wanted you to fix?
2. Of the tips listed, are there any that you did not know were a problem for your spouse?
3. Is it more likely that you would work on something if you knew your spouse wanted it?
4. Are there things that you want but you will not share with your spouse? If so, explain.
5. How has holding back on things affected your relationship? Has it helped or hurt it? Explain?
6. Explain how you feel when your spouse works on the things you've requested.
7. Explain how you feel when your spouse refuses to work on the things you've requested.
8. How important is it that your spouse keep their word?
9. Are either of you overly critical of the other, if so in what areas?
10. As a couple what is your strategy for providing for each other in these areas?

Exercise:

If you are not spiritually mature enough to handle this exercise then please don't do it.
Take an opportunity to talk freely about the things you want from each other. This must be done without anger or any fear of reprisal. There can be no shouting or bitterness only honest requests and desires. There can be no judging. You can each take a turn. One round is when both of you have had a chance to speak and listen. There can be as many or as few rounds as you see fit. (Maybe three or five would be a good place to start).

Sentences should begin with a compliment and then a request. "I love you for __________, or I appreciate you for _________." If you could I would also appreciate it if you would ___________________. Another one might be, "I feel ________________ when you ____________." But when you ____________ it makes me feel ___________________."
Each person should be allowed to speak uninterrupted and without the necessity of defending themselves for their statements. Neither should any defense be made of how one is presently behaving and already doing what is requested. If they were receiving it they wouldn't request it.

NOTES

NOTES

Chapter Twenty

The Couple That ________ Together

DISCUSSION QUESTIONS:

1. Discuss the concept that marriage is our story.
2. Are you and your spouse writing separate stories and is this the problem in your marriage?
3. Explain God's design in marriage in terms of togetherness?
4. What are some other relationships where togetherness is essential to success?
5. What might be some causes as to how people start together and drift apart?
6. How can we prevent our oneness from becoming a divided house?
7. Can we write our story if our personalities are different?
8. When couples drift apart how does that impact their relationship with God?
9. If you examined yourself would you find that you've contributed to the drifting apart?
10. What are you willing to do to make sure you and your spouse remain one?

Exercise:

Take the time to pray together about your relationship. Begin by asking God for forgiveness; if you have drifted apart from each other you have likely drifted from God. Ask God to come back to the center of your marriage. Study the triangle with God at the top and the couple at each corner at the bottom. The distance between us is greatest from each other when we are the farthest from God. As we move closer to God we move closer to each other.

Take a piece of paper and write down the things we are together on and the things on which we are apart. Examine the things we are apart on and discuss why we are apart. Don't yell or accuse. Explain and listen. Bring Scripture to bear on the subject when appropriate and allow God to tell us the truth and then make sure both of you agree with God.

NOTES

NOTES

Bonus Exercise

A New Vow

Each person needs a piece of paper, preferably the same kind of paper-lined or not. It doesn't matter, but use the same kind and a pen or pencil. You can't use an electronic device for this exercise, you will need a piece of paper.

Open your Bible and read Matthew 7:12 together. As you read the verse imagine you are having a conversation with Jesus. This verse is Jesus asking you personally, how you would like for people to treat you.
You both need to be honest with Jesus because of course he already knows our hearts.

After reading the verse, write down the ways in which you would tell Jesus you want people to treat you. Do you want honesty, respect, love, mercy, forgiveness etc. Answer for yourself and don't allow your spouse to see your answers.

Once you both are finished share your answers with each other. If some are the same, that is fine-we would expect some of them to be. After you share your answers with each other sign your name at the bottom of your paper.

Now we are ready for the exercise. After signing your name give your paper to your spouse and declare to them that you will do for them what you wrote that you wanted done for you. Jesus asked you you want people to treat you. He then said, "Now you go do that for them."

Now that you have signed your names, switched papers and declared your intentions and willingness to do what you wrote for your spouse, frame your papers and hang the frames in your house as a constant reminder of your new vows to each other. Teach your children what the framed words mean and share with your family and friends who enter your home. Your marriage will be an example to others, God will be glorified and you will be blessed.

Remember the words of Jesus - happy are you if you do them.

Conclusion

Marriage is arguably the greatest gift God has given us. It is a journey designed to take us from earth to heaven. We chose this person to walk through life with, we found each other, told our friends and family and all who would hear how much we loved each other. We invited them to attend our wedding and stood before God and witnesses and took vows demonstrating our love and commitment.

Then challenges came and we found ourselves struggling to keep our word. But we can get back, in fact we can become better. You have the right spouse you made the right choice. Let's go back to the God who gave us marriage. Let's return to the all wise ruler of heaven and earth and let's live like him.

Let's take God and take back our marriage.

May God bless you and may God bless your marriage.

Other Books By Eric L. Owens Available at www.EricLOwens.com

So You Want To Be Happy

So You Want To Be Happy Teens

Do You Take God?

Connect with Eric on his blog, www.EricLOwens.com.

Facebook: www.facebook.com/soyouwanttobehappy

Made in the USA
San Bernardino, CA
31 October 2018